CHESS

FROM FIRST MOVES TO CHECKMATE

CHESS

FROM FIRST MOVES TO CHECKMATE

Daniel King

KINGFISHER

NEW YORK

KINGFISHER
LONDON & NEW YORK

Text copyright © 2000 by Daniel King
Copyright © 2000 by Kingfisher
Published in the United States by Kingfisher,
175 Fifth Ave., New York, NY 10010
Kingfisher is an imprint of Macmillan Children's Books, London.
All rights reserved.

Distributed in the U.S. by Macmillan, 175 Fifth Ave., New York, NY 10010
Distributed in Canada by H.B. Fenn and Company Ltd., 34 Nixon Road, Bolton, Ontario L7E 1W2

Library of Congress Cataloging-in-Publication data has been applied for.

ISBN: 978-0-7534-1930-4

Kingfisher books are available for special promotions and premiums. For details contact:
Special Markets Department, Macmillan, 175 Fifth Avenue, New York, NY 10010.

For more information, please visit www.kingfisherpublications.com

First published in 2000
This new edition published in 2010

Printed in China
1 3 5 7 9 8 6 4 2
1TR/0709/LFA/MAR(MAR)128MA/C

CONTENTS

PART ONE

INTRODUCTION

Introduction 6
The Evolving Game 8

CHESS BASICS

Setting Up 10
The King 12
The Rook 13
The Bishop 14
The Queen 15
The Knight 16
The Pawn 17
Notation 18
Check and Checkmate I 20
Check and Checkmate II 22
Material Chess 24
Special Moves 26

INTO BATTLE

Opening the Game 28
Forks, Pins, and Skewers 30
Four Lethal Attacks 32
Sacrifice! 34

What Is a Draw? 36
Training Exercises 38
Test Positions 40

PART TWO

THE WORLD OF CHESS

The World Championship I 42
The World Championship II 44
The Greatest 46
The Shortest and Longest Games 48
Starers and Shakers 50
The Russians and Chess 52
Computers and Chess 54
The Ultimate Challenge 56

REFERENCE

Glossary 58
Answers and Resources 60

Index 62
Acknowledgments 64

This ancient Egyptian illustration shows that people have been playing board games for thousands of years.

INTRODUCTION

Chess is a game of war. You control one army and your opponent, the enemy, controls the other. The fate of your army depends entirely on your own skill. Most other games rely on chance—a move may be determined by a roll of the dice, or the turn of a card. But in chess there is no luck. You are entirely responsible for your own success or failure, and this is why chess can be one of the most satisfying of all games to win.

THE ULTIMATE GAME

Before you make a move on the chessboard you must try to predict, as far as you can, how your opponent will react. In deciding what to play, you will need to use reason, memory, and logic combined with a dash of intuition and inspiration.

It has been claimed that there are more possible moves on the chessboard than there are atoms in the universe. This helps account for the game's popularity through the ages. Chess has never been "solved." Even in today's computer age, it remains as complex and fascinating as it must have been when it emerged in India, almost 1,500 years ago.

▷ From the 700s until the 1000s, the Islamic world produced the best chess players. The Arabs were the first players to record their moves. Many of these games survive to this day.

"Chess is life in miniature. Chess is struggle, chess is battles." Garry Kasparov World Chess Champion, 1985–2000

THE ORIGINS OF CHESS

No one knows how the game of chess began. It is not clear whether it was invented by one person, or whether several different games gradually merged into one. Board games have been played for at least 6,000 years, but the game we recognize as chess can be traced back to 7th-century India. Its roots probably go back further. The game may even have emerged from a religious ceremony held in order to divine the balance between good and evil.

From northern India, chess spread quickly to Persia, and after the Arabian conquest during the 600s, it reached the Arab world. Chess thrived in the Golden Age of Islam between the 700s and the 1000s. The Arabs were great mathematicians, and the geometric nature of chess complemented their scientific interests.

Chess arrived in Europe by a variety of different trade routes, as well as through the Moorish invasion of Spain in the 700s, and the Islamic conquest of Sicily not long after. The Vikings took the game farther westward. By the beginning of the 1000s, chess was already well known across Europe.

◁▷ The Isle of Lewis chess pieces date back to about the 1100s. They form the oldest surviving complete set. The pieces are carved from walrus ivory and depict characters in a variety of bad moods—from rage to gloom.

◁ Chess came to Europe from the Arab world along trade routes and through conquest. In a short period of time it became the most popular board game in Europe.

△ *The earliest European study of chess is a Spanish work that dates from the late 1200s.*

▽ *When this Italian picture of two chess-playing sisters was painted in 1555, the rules of the game had settled into the ones we know today.*

THE EVOLVING GAME

During the later Middle Ages, between 1100 and 1450, chess established itself as the most popular board game in Europe—among the ruling classes. It was not until the 1900s that chess became a game played by millions of ordinary people.

A MIRROR OF SOCIETY

The names of the pieces that we use today—the king, queen, bishop, and knight—were established during the Middle Ages, when society was very ordered and geared toward warfare. Chess reflected this rigid world, and it found a place in many ballads and poems of the period.

DYNAMIC CHANGES

After the 1450s, during the period known as the Renaissance, the rules of chess evolved into the ones used today. As society and cultural life became more dynamic, so did chess. The queen, until then a piece with limited powers, now became the most powerful piece on the board. The bishop also extended its range, and pawns were permitted to move two squares on the first move. These rule changes meant that a lightning attack was possible right from the very beginning of the game.

CHESS ON THE MOVE

Many different cultures and places have produced great chess players over the centuries. In the Renaissance, Spain and Italy were the strongest chess-playing nations. From the middle of the 1700s, Paris produced many excellent players, and in the middle of the 1800s, when the British Empire was at its height, London became the center of chess life. In the early 1900s, chess ceased to be a game played exclusively by the idle rich. As chess became more democratic, centers of excellence sprang up all over the world—in central Europe (Berlin, Vienna, Budapest), in the Soviet Union, and in North and South America. Chess had truly become a game for everyone.

LIVING HISTORY

In the long and varied history of chess, each generation has built upon the experience and knowledge of the preceding one. Records of the game have survived through the ages—they let us trace a clear line of thinking that goes right back to the earliest days of the game. Whenever you play chess you are taking part in an ancient activity and making a direct link with players who lived almost 1,500 years ago.

Did you know ?

One of the first books printed in English was The Game and Playe of the Chesse, *in 1474. It was written by William Caxton.*

△ *During the 1800s, chess clubs sprang up across Europe. Matches took place in coffeehouses, important social meeting places at this time.*

△ *Today, chess is played by millions of people across the world. Its popularity is such that movies are made about the competitive game.*

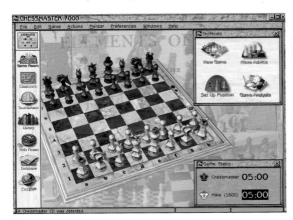

△ *Computer chess has been a major innovation of the past three decades. Powerful chess-playing programs let you play against the machine and are a great way to improve your game.*

◁ *During the long history of chess, the different pieces have inspired a wide variety of designs. These examples come from 18th-century Germany, 19th-century China, and 20th-century Italy.*

9

SETTING UP

King	Queen	Rook	Bishop	Knight	Pawn

Chess is a game played by two players on a board of 64 squares, half of them white (or a pale color) and the other half black (or dark). One player commands the white pieces, the other the black pieces, taking turns to move. White always makes the first move at the beginning of the game.

When positioning the board at the beginning of the game, make sure there is a white square in the lower right-hand corner. Besides being part of the rules, this helps you set up the pieces for the beginning of the game.

The pieces are always set up in exactly the same way for the start of the game. On the first row of squares (or "rank") stand the most important pieces. The rooks—sometimes called castles—sit in the corners. Next to them on both sides of the board are the knights. Then come the bishops, and finally, on the middle two squares, stand the king and queen.

Be sure to put the king and queen on the right squares. There is an easy rule to help you do this—the queen stands on its own color. In other words, if you have a White queen it will be placed on the white square nearest the middle. If you have a Black queen it will stand on the black square nearest the middle. In front of these pieces, on the second rank, is a row of eight pawns.

Pieces should always be placed in the middle of the squares. Only one piece is allowed per square at a time. However, enemy pieces can be captured by moving onto a square that they occupy.

◁ In this book the chessboard and pieces are often represented by a simple diagram. If you are not sure which piece is which, you can refer back to the page opposite.

1

2

Test position

Which pieces can the White king take? Answer on page 60.

♔ THE KING

The king is easy to recognize. In most chess sets it is the tallest piece, and it always has a small cross on top of its crown.

The king is the most important piece on the chessboard. The whole game revolves around the struggle to trap the king. This is called checkmate. Lose this piece and you lose the game, so it is vital to keep the king as secure as possible. It is usually best to tuck the king away at the side of the board and surround it with a protective shield of pawns—just as political leaders in real life are protected by bodyguards. If a king loses the cover of its pieces, it is likely to fall prey to an attack by the enemy army because it cannot move out of danger very quickly.

The king may be the most important piece, but it is actually one of the least powerful. It is only allowed to move one square at a time, although it may move in any direction. It can capture other pieces, but it cannot move to a square where it might be captured, or put in check. For now, just try to learn, memorize, and practice the basic moves (**diagrams 1 and 2**).

There is also one special move, or leap, that the king can make just once in the game. It is called castling, and it is explained on page 26.

Did you know?

Chess is sometimes known as the Royal Game. Kings and queens have played chess for centuries, including the English king William the Conqueror, who is said to have broken a chessboard over a French prince's head.

THE ROOK

1

At the start of the game you have two rooks in your army of pieces. They stand at the corners of the board and look like the turrets of a castle. Some players call them "castles," although the proper name is rook.

Rooks are powerful pieces, but at the beginning of the game they are unable to move at all because they are hemmed in by the other pieces. They really come into their own later on, when the game has opened up.

Rooks can move up and down and side to side on the board, unless there is something blocking their path. They cannot leap over other pieces, except when they perform the special move of "castling" (*see page 26*).

In this position (**diagram 1**), the rook can move to any of the squares marked by the arrows. Compare the mobility of the rook to the limited range of the king. It is like the difference between a tortoise and a hare.

2

The rook can zoom from one side of the board to the other, but only if there is nothing in its way. Here, for instance, it cannot move past the White king (**diagram 2**).

Did you know ?

The word "rook" derives from an old Arabic word, rukh, meaning chariot. By the time chess reached Europe, sometime after A.D. 700, chariots were no longer in use. So the rook came to resemble a castle's turret, which more accurately reflected the nature of society and warfare during the Middle Ages.

Test position

Which pieces can the White rook take? Answer on page 60.

①

②

Test position

Which pieces can the White bishop take? Answers on page 60.

♗ THE BISHOP

Next to the king and queen at the start of the game you will find the bishops. This reflects their status in medieval society, when the clergy were at the heart of government and crucial advisors to the ruling monarchs.

The bishop may move forward or backward along a diagonal path for as many squares as it likes, as long as no pieces of its own color stand in its way. The bishop can move to any of the squares along the lines of the arrows (**diagram 1**).

Both sides have two bishops, one that runs along the dark squares of the board, the other on the light squares. A bishop that begins on a white square can only move along the white squares. A bishop that begins on a black square must stay on the black squares (**diagram 2**).

A "bishop pair" can be very powerful in an open position, exerting influence right across the board. They are often best placed at the edges, far away from attacking enemy pieces, but still able to make their presence felt across the center and the opposite side of the board.

Did you know ?

When the game of chess began in India, the bishops were known as "elephants." In many languages the name still survives to this day. In Russian, for example, the word slon, which means elephant, is used to refer to the bishop.

THE QUEEN

The queen is easy to recognize—it always has a crown at the top of the piece, and is just a bit shorter than the king, which it stands next to at the start of the game.

①

The queen is able to move up and down and across the board like a rook, as well as along the diagonals like a bishop, as long as there is nothing blocking its path. When it is in the center of the board the queen exercises extraordinary power (**diagram 1**).

The queen does not have to stand in the middle of the board in order to have a decisive impact on the game. Even from the corner, the queen's influence stretches right across to the other side of the board. The queen is able to move to any of the squares along the marked arrows (**diagram 2**).

②

Although the king is the most important piece in your army, the queen is actually the most powerful. This means that you should take good care of this piece—if the queen is lost, defeat is often inevitable. Try not to move the queen out too early in the game. First, make sure you have found a safe square for it.

Did you know ?

In the original game in India and Persia, this piece—the "vizier"—actually had very limited powers. However, after the 1400s, the queen became a more powerful piece, in keeping with a changing and more dynamic society.

Test position

Which pieces can the White queen take? Answers on page 60.

1

2

Test position

Which pieces can the Black knight take? Answers on page 60.

THE KNIGHT

The knight is one of the craftiest members of your army. It has the unique ability to leap over other pieces. This, combined with its sidestepping movement, can make it a difficult piece to deal with.

The knight moves two squares in a straight direction, and then one to the side, either to the left or the right. It might be easier if you think of the move as a kind of L-shape (**diagram 1**).

The knight makes the game more dynamic. In positions that appear blocked it can force a breakthrough because it is the only chess piece that is able to leap over other pieces. Here, for instance, it can capture the bishop that stands on the other side of the pawns (**diagram 2**).

Because the knight is a short-range piece, it often functions poorly at the side or the corner of the board, where its scope is limited. You will find that it is much more effective to keep your knights in the middle of the board, where they have more options.

Did you know ?

As far as we know, the "L-shaped" knight move has remained the same since the beginnings of the game in early 7th-century India. This leaping piece has always been associated with the cavalry.

THE PAWN

Eight pawns stand in front of your other pieces. They are the foot soldiers, the least valuable members of your army. Nevertheless, they still perform a very important role in the game.

On their first move, pawns are able to advance either two squares, or one. After this, they are only allowed to move forward one square at a time (**diagram 1**). They cannot move backward or sideways. Among other duties, pawns are used to mark out territory before the most important pieces advance into battle.

Unlike all other pieces, pawns progress straight up the board, but they capture one square diagonally forward. The other pieces capture in the same direction that they move. Here, for instance, White could choose to take either the rook or the knight (**diagram 2**).

Pawns have one special property that can prove decisive in many games. If a pawn reaches the other side of the board, it must immediately transform into another piece—a knight, bishop, rook, or queen (**diagram 3**). In practice, most people choose a new queen because it is the most powerful piece on the board. Promoting a pawn occurs most frequently at the end of the game, when there are fewer pieces to obstruct the progress of the pawn down the board.

Did you know ?

In the 1700s, the French player André Philidor called pawns "the soul of chess." He recognized that pawns, despite their limited mobility, can often determine the nature and outcome of a game.

1

2

3

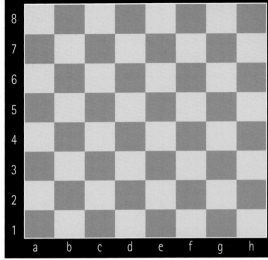

The rows of squares going up the board, the files, are each given a letter, from a to h. The rows of squares across the board are known as ranks. These are given a number from 1 to 8. Using this system, it is easy to identify each square on the chessboard with a letter and a number.

NOTATION

Chess games from hundreds of years ago survive to this day because the moves were recorded. In the past, a variety of methods were used to note the moves, but it is the "algebraic system" that now predominates throughout the world.

ALGEBRAIC NOTATION

"Algebraic notation" sounds far more complicated than it actually is. If you have ever found a place on a map, then you will already be familiar with the system. Algebraic notation is based on a simple grid system of eight letters and eight numbers. By combining a letter with a number, it makes it very easy to identify each square, as the diagrams on this page show.

It is important to learn chess notation if you want to understand the many diagrams in this book, or to read other chess books and magazines. Later, you will also be able to record your games for posterity!

For example, the square in the bottom right-hand corner is known as h1—the letter is always put before the number. No matter which side of the board you are on, the numbers and letters remain the same. The h1 square is always in White's bottom right-hand corner.

1 Take a look at this position. The rook moves up the board and Black responds by moving a pawn. These moves would be recorded in the following way—**1 Rd7 c6**.

2 The **1** is the move number, the **R** stands for the rook, **d7** identifies the square the rook moves to. Black's move is given in the second column. The pawn moves to the **c6** square. Pawns are not identified by a letter—only the square they move to is recorded.

Except for the pawn, each piece is identified by a single capital letter:

K	King	To avoid confusion with the king, the knight is given the letter **N**. The pieces are always identified with capital letters. For the squares, lowercase letters are used.
Q	Queen	
R	Rook	
B	Bishop	
N	Knight	

Here is a simple test. Set your pieces up for the start of the game and play out the following moves on your board (the **x** indicates a capture and the **+** means check).

1 e4 c5
2 Nf3 d6
3 d4 cxd4
4 Nxd4 Nf6
5 Bb5+ Nbd7

You should have reached the position in diagram 3.

3 On the third move, notice that when Black's pawn captures, the file it comes from is noted (an exception to the rule that only the destination of the piece is recorded). In this case the pawn was on the c-file, and it captured a piece on the d4 square, so it is written **3 ...cxd4**. (The three dots are a standard convention to indicate that this is Black's move, not White's.) On the fifth move, both of Black's knights could move to the d7 square, therefore a b is used to indicate which one goes there—in this case the knight standing on the b-file.

White's king is being attacked by the rook. We say that the king is in check. According to the rules of the game, the king must move out of check immediately. Here, there is only one option—to move one square up the board.

1

CHECK AND CHECKMATE I

Now that you know how the pieces move, it is time to tackle the principles of check and checkmate.

Checkmating your opponent's king is the ultimate aim in a chess game. The term comes from the ancient Persian "shah mat," meaning "the king is defeated." You have to threaten the enemy king with one of your pieces so that it is unable to move and escape capture. A checkmate usually occurs when one side's forces—or "army"—are overwhelmingly superior, or by a direct and unexpected assault on the king.

Checking is a little different. It occurs when the king is attacked by a piece, but can still escape. In other words, it is not necessarily fatal. The positions illustrated above demonstrate what the terms mean.

This time, the position has changed a little. White's king is again in check from the rook, but now there is no escape. The king is trapped by its own pieces and cannot move out of check, so we say it is checkmated. The game is over and White has lost!

2

WHAT IS THE ADVANTAGE OF CHECKING?

Don't panic if your opponent suddenly thumps down a piece and cries "check." It does not end the game, and it does not always benefit your opponent. So what exactly is the point of checking?

- A check can help you gain time.
- Checking can drive the enemy king to a weak square, making it vulnerable to further attack.

TEST POSITIONS

To make sure you understand the concepts of check and checkmate, here are six test positions for you to solve. You have to figure out if it is check or checkmate, and if it is only check, how do you escape? The solutions are on the next two pages, but before turning to them, try solving the positions first.

Did you know ?

If you fail to spot that you are in check, and do not prevent the attack on your king, it does not necessarily mean that you have lost the game. Your opponent has to let you take your move back. You must then play another move that gets you out of the check.

1 *(Black to play)*
Is this check or checkmate?

2 *(Black to play)*
Is this check or checkmate?

3 *(White to play)*
Is this check or checkmate?

4 *(Black to play)*
Is this check or checkmate?

5 *(White to play)*
Is this check or checkmate?

6 *(White to play)*
Is this check or checkmate?

1 *In this position, Black has been checkmated. White's knight is directly attacking the king, but the king is unable to escape because it is smothered by its own pieces.*

2 *Black has been checkmated here, too. The king is trapped in the corner and is in check from White's queen. It cannot take the queen, which is protected by the rook standing on g1.*

3 *White has been checkmated. The king is in check from the rook and cannot escape. It cannot move to b3 or b1—the knight has both squares covered.*

4 *Black's king is in check from the bishop, but it is not checkmate. The Black king can get out of danger by moving one square to the side.*

CHECK AND CHECKMATE II —ANSWERS

The last three positions demonstrate the three methods of getting out of check—by moving the king, blocking the check, or capturing the piece that is checking.

When you are trying to figure out how to get out of check, remember these three key words—*move*, *block*, and *capture*.

5 *White is in check but it is not checkmate. It is possible to advance the pawn on g2 one square to block the queen's check. Black would then be ill-advised to take the pawn on g3 with the queen —it is protected by the pawn on h2.*

6 *Black's queen is checking White's king in the corner of the board. However, it is not checkmate because White's rook can take Black's queen, leaving White with an overwhelming advantage.*

MATERIAL CHESS

Checkmating your opponent is the ultimate aim in a game of chess. But what is the best strategy to achieve this goal?

You will often find that your opponent's king is surrounded by a wall of pieces. When this happens a direct attack might not succeed. This is when a more effective strategy known as "material chess" comes into play.

In most cases, for a checkmating attack to succeed, you need to have a superiority of forces. So, at first, your strategy should be to protect your own army. At the same time you should also be thinking of ways to trap and take your opponent's pieces. It is not advisable to go after the enemy king until you have a greater number of pieces than your opponent. So before each move, you need to ask yourself two important questions:

1) Can I capture any enemy pieces?

2) Are any of my pieces threatened?

Take a look at the following positions, keeping the above questions in mind.

1 *Imagine that you are White. Is Black threatening to take any of your pieces? Can you capture any of Black's?*

2 *There are no threats from Black, so White is free to send the queen to the other side of the board and capture Black's knight.*

3 *Imagine you are Black. Are any of your pieces under attack? Can you capture any of White's pieces?*

4 *None of Black's pieces are threatened, so you are free to make an attack. There is a pawn on the b4 square that the bishop can take:* **1 ...Bxb4.** *Black has won a pawn.*

5 *You may have noticed that Black can make another capture in diagram 3. The queen can take White's bishop on e3. Isn't it better to grab a bishop rather than a pawn?*

6 *Not in this case. White would then be able to capture the queen, winning a decisive advantage in pieces.*

The last example (**diagram 6**) leads us to an important aspect of chess—how much each piece is actually worth. The value of each piece is based on its power on the board. Remembering these values will help you decide which pieces to exchange, and which pieces to keep.

The queen, with its ability to move like a rook and a bishop, is by far the most powerful piece on the board. It therefore has the highest value: 9 points. Next comes the rook with 5 points. The bishop and the knight are both worth 3 points, and finally comes the lowly pawn, worth just one point. Remember that these are just rough values. In some positions a bishop is far more effective than a knight—and vice versa. Even so, they provide a useful guide when we are trying to make a tricky decision in the heat of the battle.

For example, in the last diagram, it would make no sense to capture the bishop with the queen. White would gain a queen worth nine points, and only lose a bishop worth just three points. A good rate of exchange for White—but not for Black!

You will often win a game by first capturing more pieces than your opponent. You can then wear your enemy down to an endgame. At this stage of the game you are more likely to be in a position to promote a pawn into a new queen; only then can you launch an attack on the king.

But remember, chess games are not won just by gathering enemy pieces. Don't lose sight of the ultimate goal—checkmate!

VALUE

9

5

3

3

1

SPECIAL MOVES

There is one special move during a game when both the king and the rook can leave their starting squares on the same turn. This move is called castling. It can be a highly effective way of protecting your king.

Castling brings the king, your most important piece, to a safe place at the side of the board. It also enables one of your most powerful pieces, the rook, to enter the game. All this with just one move!

You can castle on both sides of the board. Kingside castling (**diagrams 1 and 2**) is also known as "short castling." Queenside castling (**diagrams 3 and 4**) is called "long castling" because there are more squares between the king and the rook on this side of the board.

1

The king moves two squares to the right along the first rank, and the rook leaps over and lands on the square next to it.

2

After castling, the king is now at the side of the board. This is a much safer position than in the middle.

It is also possible to castle on the other side of the board. Once again, the king moves two squares along the first rank, this time to the left, and the rook leaps over and next to the king on the other side.

3

This is known as queenside castling, or long castling. Notice that the king is not as deep in the corner as it is in kingside castling.

4

THE RULES OF CASTLING

Castling may seem a little tricky at first, but try to familiarize yourself with the rules as quickly as possible because this is such a vital move.

- You cannot castle if your king has already moved.

- You cannot castle if your rook has already moved.

- You cannot castle if your king is in check on that turn.

- You cannot castle if your king lands into a check.

- Your king cannot castle through the line of another piece.

- You cannot castle if there is a piece standing in the way of the king or rook.

Here is an example of castling (**diagrams 5 and 6**) that should help make things clear.

EN PASSANT

It's not only the rook and king that can make a special move. There is also an unusual kind of pawn capture, which is only available in a particular situation (**see diagrams 7 and 8**). The rule, which is known as "en passant," is a legacy from 500 years ago, when pawns were first allowed to advance two squares on their opening move.

The "en passant" capture is available only when a pawn advances two squares from its starting position on a file adjacent to an enemy pawn on the fifth rank.

5 *Black's king is under severe pressure from White's rooks and queen in the middle of the board. It's time to evacuate the king from the center. Black cannot castle on the kingside—the king is not allowed to move through the line of the bishop, which covers the f8 square. However, it is possible to castle on the queenside.*

6 *A great side step by Black's king. Castling has enabled the king to move closer to the security of the corner of the board, and Black's rook, which was languishing at the side, enters the fray.*

7 *If a pawn moves out two squares from its starting position, an enemy pawn standing next to it on the fifth rank is allowed to capture it.*

8 *The White pawn moves one square diagonally behind the Black pawn, and removes it from the board. It's as if the Black pawn had only moved one square.*

If a player is to capture "en passant," it must be done on the turn immediately after the opposition pawn has moved two squares, or the option disappears.

OPENING THE GAME

Now that you have learned the basic principles of chess, you are ready to learn about the most effective ways of getting a game under way. This initial phase of the game is known as the opening.

At the beginning of the game most of your pieces are boxed in. Only the pawns, which stand in front of the other pieces, can move along with the knights, which are able to leap over the pawns to the third rank.

Here are the first few moves of a game where White does all the right things, and Black makes plenty of mistakes. But we can learn from mistakes, too!

1 1 e4 e5 *Moving the pawn two squares to e4 is one of the best opening moves. The pawn not only controls crucial squares in the middle of the board, it also frees the way for the queen and bishop to enter the game. Black replies in the same way.* **2 d4**

2 *A bold central advance by White, putting pressure on Black's center and allowing the other bishop to enter the game.* **2 ...exd4 3 c3**

3 *Understandably, Black has captured the pawn in the middle of the board, and White replies by offering another! Was that wise?* **3 ...dxc3 4 Nxc3**

4 *Black grabs the second pawn and White recaptures with the knight. White is playing a "gambit." This is when a piece is given up in the opening in order to free your other pieces.* **4 ...Nc6 5 Bc4 Nf6 6 Nf3**

5 White has brought out a bishop and a knight, and Black has brought out two knights. These are all strong moves because they help control important squares in the center of the board. **6 ...Qe7 7 0-0** *(This is how kingside castling is recorded.)*

6 Black's last move was dubious. The queen is in danger of being attacked by less valuable pieces, so for the moment it should not be moved. White's last move was excellent. Castling brings the king to the side of the board, where it is protected by a row of pawns, and also brings the rook into play. **7 ...Nxe4**

7 Black falls for a trap! Another pawn is taken, but this opens the center, leaving the king in great danger. **8 Nxe4 Qxe4 9 Re1**

8 A total disaster for Black. The queen is attacked by the rook but is unable to move away because the king would then be in check. In other words, the queen will be lost. We say that the queen is "pinned" to the king (there is more on the tactic of "pinning" on pages 30-31).

White did well, but Black's play was poor. There are three opening principles that should be kept in mind when playing the first few moves of the game.

1 Control the center
If you control the center of the board, then you control the game. You will also find it easier to deal with any difficulties as the game develops.

2 Bring out your pieces
On the chessboard it is vital that your entire army comes into play as quickly as possible. If your pieces are too slow, the battle could be lost before you know it.

3 Castle
Remember, your king is the most important piece, but at the same time, one of the least powerful. By castling as quickly as possible, it can be put in a safe position. You will also find that bringing the rook from the corner into play can be very useful in the fight for the center.

DANGER!
Do not move your queen out too early in the game. It is liable to be attacked and driven back by weaker pieces. Although the queen is your most powerful piece, it still needs the support of the rest of your army.

FORKS, PINS, AND SKEWERS

Forks, pins, and skewers are some of the sneakiest tricks you can use against your opponent. These tactics can lead to winning one, and sometimes several, enemy pieces, and, ultimately, to winning the game.

Although it is unlikely that you will find the positions on the opposite page duplicated exactly in your own games, you will soon begin to recognize similar positions. The more you play, the more familiar you will become with these highly effective and often deadly moves.

THE FORK
This is a simultaneous attack on two enemy pieces. The most common fork is made by the knight (**diagram 1**). Knight forks feature in many games, so it is important to familiarize yourself with the move—for your own safety! Pawns can also make effective two-pronged attacks (**diagram 2**). The bishop and the knight are frequently the target of pawn forks.

THE PIN
The pin is an attack against two enemy pieces standing on the same line. Like the fork, this is also extremely common. We have already encountered a pin on page 29 (**diagram 8**). On that occasion, a rook pinned the queen to the king. This time (**diagrams 3 and 4**) the pin is a little different.

THE SKEWER
This can be a deadly maneuver. The skewer attack operates by piercing through one piece to trap another standing on the same rank, file, or diagonal. The second piece is the real target (**diagrams 5 and 6**).

1 White's knight has leaped in, checking Black's king, and at the same time attacking the queen. Lethal! Black must move the king out of check, then the knight captures the queen on the next turn.

2 This is another example of a fork, this time by a pawn. Black's pawn has just advanced, simultaneously attacking the bishop and the knight. One of the pieces can be saved, but not both, so Black wins material. (Remember, a pawn is worth just one point and the bishop and knight three.)

3 Here is a very effective pin. Black's bishop has moved out to attack the queen. White's queen cannot escape because the king would then be in check. The best that White can do is take the bishop with the queen—but then lose this key piece to the Black knight on the following move.

4 In this position, White's pawn moves up to attack the knight in a classic case of how to exploit a pin. If Black's knight moves, then the queen will be taken by the rook. There is no escape—the capture of Black's knight has become inevitable.

5 A skewer can be a deadly piece of playing. Here, Black's king is in check from White's queen. The king must move out of check. White's queen will then capture Black's queen.

6 White's rook has just moved to b5, attacking the queen. The queen must move because it is Black's most valuable piece. But when it does, White's rook can capture the exposed knight.

Four Lethal Attacks

There are many cunning and devious ways to make an attack. Some occur with such frequency that they have been given specific names—as we have just seen. Here are a few more lethal weapons to add to your armory.

DISCOVERED CHECK
Although it has a slightly confusing name (like a lot of chess jargon), this can be very effective. Discovered check is when a piece moves out of the path of another piece, which can then give check (**see diagrams 1 and 2**).

1 Look at the position of Black's rook in relation to White's king. It would be in check if it weren't for Black's knight, which sits between the two. That gives Black an idea. The knight could be moved out of the way, putting White's king in check from the rook. Now, here's the clever bit. Why not move the knight so that it attacks the queen?

DIAGONAL BATTERY
You might think that a castled king position is fairly safe. After all, it is at the side of the board, away from the exposed center, and, in this case (**diagram 3**), protected by pawns. But a castled king is not invulnerable.

3 White has craftily lined up a battery of firepower—the queen is in front of the bishop on the so-called long diagonal. In this position the White queen can inflict maximum damage.

4 Black's king cannot get out of check—the White queen is covered by the bishop. Checkmate! Here it was very easy for White to set up the battery of queen and bishop, but in the cut and thrust of battle, it may not be so simple. Even so, watch out for this deadly attack in your games.

SEVENTH HEAVEN

At the start of a game, the rooks, trapped in the corners, struggle to make their mark on the game. However, later on, when pieces have been cleared from the board, the rooks play a more prominent role, zooming down open files. If they are able to reach the seventh rank, they can be extremely dangerous, capturing pawns and pinning the enemy king to the side of the board (**diagrams 5** and **6**).

5 The two Black rooks have both made it to the seventh rank. Nothing can stop them from sweeping up everything in their path. Now they even have the chance to deliver the final blow.

6 The rook sweeps over to deliver checkmate to the helpless king, which cannot capture it because it is now defended by Black's second rook. Two rooks on the seventh rank are exceptionally powerful, but even a single rook should not be underestimated.

BACK RANK MATE

We now move from the seventh to the eighth rank—the last or "back" rank. We already know that the sooner you castle in a game, the better. However, as we've seen, you must still be careful, even after castling.

Brilliant! The knight has moved out of the way of the rook, putting White's king in check. The king must get out of check, then on the next turn Black's knight takes the queen, the most powerful piece on the board. This will leave Black with a rook and a knight against a lone king—more than enough pieces to force a checkmate.

7 Black's rook has just moved to c8, threatening to capture the queen. At first glance, the move looks safe, since the bishop covers the rook. But White has spotted that the back rank is vulnerable and sacrifices the queen: **1 Qxc8+**. Black must recapture with the bishop: **1 ...Bxc8**. Then the rook rockets to the eighth rank: **2 Re8**.

8 It's checkmate. Black's king is unable to escape from the rook's check—it is blocked in by its own pawns. Checkmate could have been avoided by pushing out one of the pawns in front of the castled king (as White has done in this position), so that the king has an escape route if there is ever a check on the eighth rank.

SACRIFICE!

In chess, a sacrifice is when a piece is given up for greater gain. For example, it may result in winning enemy pieces or, in the best case, even forcing a checkmate.

The word "sacrifice" has associations with ancient religion—animals were once sacrificed on the altar to appease a god. You should keep in mind why a sacrifice is made—for the greater good of the community, in this case, your army of chess pieces, and the ultimate goal of checkmate. Making a sacrifice can also be a major element of surprise. Just as in a real battle, surprise is one of the most useful weapons at your disposal.

Making a sacrifice is thrilling, but it is also risky. For instance, you may miscalculate, so that when the smoke clears, the balance is negative—you are left with fewer pieces than your opponent. It is important, therefore, to weigh up the options carefully before committing yourself.

1 White has two rooks storming down a file, but so far Black's defenses are holding firm. But now comes the knockout punch. **1 Qxh7+** Shocking! White sacrifices the queen for just one pawn. Black has no alternative but to capture: **1 ...Kxh7**.

Did you know ?

In the history of chess, the greatest exponent of the sacrifice was the Latvian Mikhail Tal (1936-1992). He was able to conjure up an attack from nowhere by playing the most unexpected sacrifices. Here Tal (White) threw a knight into the middle of the board, inviting his opponent to capture it with the pawn. He realized that in return for the piece, the full force of the bishops would be unleashed on Black's king. In the end, Tal's opponent was unable to resist the pressure of the attack and lost the game.

2 *And now we see the point. Black's king has been brought out into the open so that White is now able to play:* **2 Rh4.** *Checkmate. Superb. White's rook checks the king, which has no escape—the other rook covers the only potential flight square. It is no consolation at the end of the game that Black still has its queen.*

Not all sacrifices are as dramatic as this first example. Often they are played just to win some enemy pieces. Diagrams 3 and 4 show a typical case in which White gives up a rook (worth 5 points) for a bishop (worth only 3) but the investment is repaid.

3 *White, with two extra pawns, is already doing well, but the easiest way to finish the game is to play* **1 Rxf8+.** *Black's king then takes the rook* **1 ...Kxf8.** *The point of the sacrifice is to set up a knight fork—Black's king has been forced to the perfect square:* **2 Nd7+.** *Black's king must now move out of check.*

4 **2 ...Ke7 3 Nxb8.** *The Knight captures the rook on b8, leaving White in a winning position. One of the pawns can eventually be forced to the eighth rank, making a new queen.*

Let's check the balance at the end of this skirmish. White gave up a rook (worth 5 points), but gained a rook and bishop (worth 5 and 3 points). White came out on top.

35

WHAT IS A DRAW?

When you play a game of chess, winning and losing are not the only possible outcomes. If neither side is able to force a checkmate, then the game is a draw. In serious tournament play, about half of all games end this way.

Just because a game is drawn, it does not mean that it has not been hard-fought; it is inevitable that sometimes an immovable force meets an irresistible object! There are a number of ways in which a game may end in a draw.

INSUFFICIENT MATING MATERIAL
If neither side has enough pieces left at the end of the game, then the position is declared drawn (see diagram 1).

1 *For instance, here, the game is drawn because it is impossible to checkmate with just a lone bishop— you can try if you like, but you won't get anywhere! Likewise, king and knight against a king is a draw.*

A pawn is less powerful than a knight, so you might assume that king and pawn against king is also a draw—but this is not always the case. Sometimes it is possible to force the pawn to the eighth rank to get a new queen, and it is possible to checkmate with a king and queen. It is also possible to checkmate with a king and rook.

REPETITION OF POSITION
If the same position occurs three times in a game, then the player whose move it is can claim a draw (diagrams 2 and 3).

Black, with three extra pawns, is hoping for a win. However, White can force a draw. Black's king is in check from the queen, so it must move. The king moves back one square: 1 ...Kg8. White continues pursuing the king: 2 Qd8+.

2

❸

STALEMATE

Stalemate is something to watch out for when one side has an overwhelming superiority in forces, and is moving in for a checkmate against an exposed king. Stalemate is when a player cannot make any legal moves but is not in check (**diagrams 4, 5, and 6**).

❹ *With an extra queen against a lone king, White is hoping for a swift checkmate. White closes in with the queen for the kill, but comes a little too close. Black's king has no legal moves. However, this does not mean that Black is checkmated. The king is not in check—this is the crucial difference. This position is "stalemate" and is a draw.*

❺ *This is the same position as the last one, with the crucial difference that Black has one remaining pawn. Again, White's queen closes in, and this time it is strong. Although Black's king cannot move, the position is NOT stalemate. Black still has one legal move:* **1 ...a4**, *then White's queen delivers checkmate:* **2 Qe7**.

❻ *As you can see from this position, a single pawn can make all the difference between winning and drawing.*

THE FIFTY-MOVE RULE

This is an extremely rare way of making a draw. If a piece is not captured and a pawn is not moved for 50 moves, then the game may be declared drawn. This is a very rare occurrence—games of chess are not usually so boring!

AGREEING ON A DRAW

The most common way to make a draw in serious tournament games is simply by agreement. After making a move, a player announces: "I offer a draw." This can either be accepted or declined. However, all too often draws are offered and accepted as a way of playing it safe. It is better not to get into the habit of offering draws—cutting the game short unnaturally does nothing for your chess development.

TRAINING EXERCISES

In every serious sport you need to train regularly if you want to improve your game. Chess is no exception. Just like boxers training for an important fight, the strongest chess players in the world will spend months in preparation for a World Championship final, studying their opponent's style and strategy, and working on their own game.

WORKING OUT

There are simple exercises you can practice that will be enormously beneficial. You can either find a friend to play against or, if you have a chess computer, input the positions and use the machine as your sparring partner.

It is extremely important to learn how to finish off your opponent at the end of the game—the techniques explained here will help you feel confident about winning.

Even when you are practicing these training exercises, try not to take any of your moves back. The following three-step plan will help you sharpen your chess mind.

1) Eyes   2) Brain   3) Hand

1) Look at the position carefully, paying particular attention to your opponent's last move.

2) Then figure out what you think is the correct move.

3) Only then, when you are absolutely sure of your move, do you you reach for a piece.

First of all, try checkmating with a queen and rook against a lone king (**diagram 1**). After you have tried this, take a look at the method explained below.

1 1 Ra4. *An important first move. Instead of checking, the rook restricts the king, preventing it from moving into one half of the board. Only then will it be driven back by the queen.* 1 ...Kf5 2 Qd5+ Kf6 3 Ra6+ Ke7 4 Qb7+ Ke8 5 Ra8 *You should have arrived at the following position (**diagram 2**).*

2 *Black's king is in check from the rook. It is unable to escape because the queen covers all the squares on the seventh rank. Therefore, the position is checkmate. If you have practiced this maneuver and feel you have mastered it, try the same thing but with two rooks against a king. Use the same technique, but you need to be a little more careful.*

Your next exercise is a little harder than the first. You have to force checkmate using your king and queen against a lone king. It is White to play.

TIP: It is impossible for a queen to deliver checkmate on its own. It needs the assistance of the king.

3 1 Qd4+. *It is only possible to checkmate the king at the side of the board, so first it must be driven there. The queen gives a check, forcing the king backward.* **1 ...Ke6 2 Kf4 Kf7 3 Qd6**

4 *Instead of checking the Black king (which in this case would only allow it to escape up the board), the queen restricts its movement. Black's king cannot escape across the force field created by White's queen.* **3 ...Kg7 4 Kf5**. *With Black's king trapped, it is time to bring up the henchman to assist in the finish.* **4 ...Kf7 5 Qd7+ Kf8 6 Kg6 Kg8 7 Qg7**

5 *Black's king is in check from the queen, and there are no escape squares. The queen cannot be captured because White's king supports it. (Remember that the kings cannot stand on adjacent squares.) Therefore it's checkmate. The final position clearly shows how the attacking side must use the king to force checkmate.*

When there are just a few pieces on the board, the king becomes a powerful piece—in stark contrast to its role early in the game, when it should be hidden away as quickly as possible. The next training exercise aims to develop your skill in handling the king.

6 *Both sides have just a king and four pawns each. Your play needs to be subtle and highly skilled if you are going to win. You need to capture an enemy pawn with the king, then force one of your own pawns to the eighth rank to get a new queen. Then you can force a checkmate—using the techniques above.*

If you feel like increasing the complexity of the position, add a few more pawns to each side. This exercise is an excellent way to learn how the king and pawns interact.

TEST POSITIONS

To find out how much you have learned from the first half of the book, try solving these ten test positions. You will find some easy, but others require a little bit more concentration. Try to work out the answers in your head by just studying the diagrams on these pages. If you have problems visualizing the line of play, you can always set up the positions on your chessboard. Solving chess puzzles like these is an excellent way of sharpening your skills. You will find the answers on pages 60–61.

1 Of all the possible pawn moves Black could make in this position, which is the best?

2 Black can make many different captures in this position. Which one is the best?

3 White is ready to launch a violent assault with moves such as **Re1+** or **Qxd6**. How can Black best counter White's threat?

4 White's rook is in a great position on the seventh rank. How can this be used to gain a winning material advantage?

5 It's White's turn to play. How does White get a winning advantage from this position?

6 What should Black play here?

7 White can gain a winning advantage with the next move. Can you see how?

8 Black has just moved a pawn forward, attacking White's knight. How would you respond?

9 How does White gain a winning, material advantage from this position?

10 White is four pawns down—can the situation still be saved?

▷ The World Chess Champions and the years in which they held the title.

Wilhelm Steinitz
1886–1894

Emanuel Lasker
1894–1921

José-Raoul Capablanca
1921–1927

Alexander Alekhine
1927–1935, 1937–1946

Max Euwe
1935–1937

Mikhail Botvinnik
1948–1957, 1958–1960, 1961–1963

Vassily Smyslov
1957–1958

THE WORLD CHAMPIONSHIP I

Every great chess player dreams of becoming the World Chess Champion. The winner of the fiercely fought World Championship joins an illustrious list of previous titleholders that goes back over a century.

CONTESTED BEGINNINGS

In 1866, a self-confident Austrian named Wilhelm Steinitz beat the German player Adolf Anderssen in a challenge match in London and duly proclaimed himself "World Chess Champion." There had never been an official World Champion before, and it was far from clear whether Steinitz should be the first. Then in 1883, Johannes Zukertort, a German who had won a few tournaments in Europe, pulled a similar trick, and also claimed to be "World Champion." Steinitz took offense, and a match was arranged in the United States, in 1886, with the title going to the first player to win ten games. The offical World Championship was born.

THE HIGHEST HONOR

Steinitz won the match, and since then there has been a clear line of successors to the title. World Champions are accorded a huge amount of respect in the chess world. There can be gaps of many years between World Championship matches, so when they take place they generate a great deal of excitement. The matches can take weeks and sometimes months to complete.

Mikhail Tal
1960–1961

Tigran Petrosian
1963–1969

Boris Spassky
1969–1972

Bobby Fischer
1972–1975

Anatoly Karpov
1975–1985

Garry Kasparov
1985–2000

Vladimir Kramnik
2000–2007

Viswanathan Anand
2007–

Wilhelm Steinitz (1836–1900) introduced a new positional style to the game. This Austrian player realized it was not necessary to go for an all-out attack on the king in order to win.

Emanuel Lasker (1868–1941) held the title for a record 27 years. The German was a shrewd psychologist at the chessboard, playing the man, not the board. His greatest strength lay in the middlegame.

José-Raoul Capablanca (1888–1942) was a Cuban diplomat. He favored clear, simple positions, and there was an effortless quality to his victories.

Alexander Alekhine (1892–1946) fled the Soviet Union in 1921. He studied chess obsessively, for eight hours a day. An explosive, dynamic player, he died penniless although still in possession of his title.

Max Euwe (1901–1981), a Dutch mathematician, won his first tournament when he was ten. A highly logical player, he held the title for only two years.

Mikhail Botvinnik (1911–1995) has been called the "Patriarch of Soviet Chess." He was a scientist by training, and his study of all phases of the game, including the opening, was always painstakingly detailed.

Vassily Smyslov (1921–) was born in Moscow. He was a highly effective player of the endgame. In many ways he was the natural successor to Capablanca.

Mikhail Tal (1936–1992) became World Champion at the age of 23 with a style of chess that was flashy and fearless. His clashes with fellow Soviet player Botvinnik proved highly memorable.

Tigran Petrosian (1929–1984) was born in Armenia, in the former Soviet Union. His style of play was defensive, and he was extremely hard to beat.

Boris Spassky (1937–) was born in the U.S.S.R. He had an effortless, natural style, but he could never match the dedication of his great rival, Bobby Fischer.

Bobby Fischer (1943–2008) became the youngest winner ever of the U.S. national championship at the age of 14. After he won the World Championship he dropped out of competitive chess and became a virtual recluse.

Anatoly Karpov (1951–) learned to play chess when he was four and studied with Botvinnik in Moscow. He is a great natural player, more at home defending than attacking.

Garry Kasparov (1963–) was born in Azerbaijan, in the former Soviet Union, and became the youngest World Champion ever at the age of 22. His chess is extremely dynamic and powerful.

Vladimir Kramnik (1973–) is a former pupil of Kasparov. Known as "Iceberg" for his coolness under pressure, he makes his pieces work together in perfect harmony.

Viswanathan Anand (1969–) is the first world champion ever from India. He plays seemingly without effort, rattling opponents with the speed of his moves.

THE WORLD CHAMPIONSHIP II

When a World Championship match is played, millions of chess enthusiasts follow the games. Knowing that so many people are watching can inspire the players to perform brilliantly—or to collapse completely.

Petrosian (White) gives away his queen: **30 Qh8+**. *A neat temporary sacrifice to drag Black's king onto a poor square. Spassky resigns immediately—a deadly knight fork occurs after* **30 ...Kxh8 31 Nxf7+**. *Black's king must get out of check:* **31 ...Kg7** *but then the knight takes the queen:* **32 Nxg5**.

THE BEST MOVE IN A WORLD CHAMPIONSHIP?

The standard of play in World Championship matches has been, as one would expect, incredibly high, so it is difficult to select one move above thousands. However, this is one particulary memorable move (**diagram 1**). It is from the 1966 match between Tigran Petrosian and Boris Spassky. Petrosian finishes off his opponent in style.

①

② *This leaves White with an extra knight and a pawn – at this level more than enough material advantage to force a win.*

THE WORST MOVE IN A WORLD CHAMPIONSHIP?

Besides the many great moves, there have also been a number of outright blunders. Under pressure, even the best players in the world can play some appalling moves. This miscalculation (**diagram 3**) is from the bitter world title fight in 1978 between Viktor Korchnoi, the challenger and Soviet defector, and his archenemy, Anatoly Karpov.

Although Karpov (Black) threatens a back-rank mate with his rook, this can be prevented fairly easily by moving the g-pawn, providing an escape square for the king. Instead, Korchnoi blunders. He plays **39 Ra1**, *which allows a smart finish:* **39 ...Nf3+**, *and Korchnoi resigns the game immediately. Otherwise:* **40 gxf3**, *then* **40 ...Rg6+ 41 Kh1 Nf2**.

③

TWO WORLD TITLES

Fédération Internationale des Échecs (FIDE) is the world governing body of chess. Since 1948, it has held regular contests for the world title. In 1993, however, Garry Kasparov broke away from FIDE to organize his own world championship matches, while FIDE continued to hold separate contests. With two world champions, there was great confusion. For many years, Kasparov was the best player in the world, so he had the strongest claim to the title until 2000, when Vladimir Kramnik defeated him. Meanwhile, India's Viswanathan Anand also had a claim to the number-one spot, thanks to his excellent tournament record and his victory at the FIDE World Championship in 2000.

Finally, after years of battling egos and political posturing, a unification tournament was held in Mexico in 2007. It featured all the strongest players, with Anand winning a convincing victory. But Kramnik kept fighting with words: "I have lent Anand the title temporarily." He believed that Anand could prove his superiority only by winning in match play— and this the Indian did in Bonn, Germany, in 2008, defeating Kramnik by 6½–4½. Anand had become undisputed World Champion.

△ Mikhail Botvinnik and David Bronstein sit center stage in 1951 at the Tchaikovsky Concert Hall in Moscow, battling it out for the ultimate title.

△ Vladimir Kramnik and Viswanathan Anand have been intense rivals over the chessboard. Away from the heat of battle, however, they have maintained friendly relations. That has not always been the case with other top chess players.

White's king is trapped in the corner. Checkmate.

4

INDIAN SUPERSTAR

Anand learned the moves of chess at the age of six, became national champion at 16, and won the world junior title in 1987. Although chess has its roots in India (*see page 7*), the country had never before produced a grandmaster, and he instantly became a superstar. When Anand returns home after successes abroad, crowds mob him at the airport. He features in nationwide advertising campaigns and is sponsored by one of India's leading technology companies. In 2007, he was awarded the *Padma Vibhushan*—the second-highest civilian award in India—by the nation's president.

▷ Anand enjoys huge support in his native India, but his down-to-earth personality has also made him a popular figure around the world.

THE GREATEST

In many sports, one personality stands out as "The Greatest." In boxing, most people would pick Muhammad Ali; in hockey, it would be Wayne Gretzky; and in chess, you would have to choose Garry Kasparov. In 1985, at the age of 22, he became the youngest-ever World Champion by beating Anatoly Karpov. Kasparov successfully defended his title five times. However, in 2000, he was finally defeated by his protégé Vladimir Kramnik, and in 2005, he retired from chess.

△ Garry Kasparov salutes his cheering fans moments after winning the final decisive game of the 1985 World Championship match. He was awarded the winner's wreath (above) for the first time in his career.

EARLY YEARS

Kasparov was born in 1963 to a Russian Jewish father and Armenian mother in Baku, Azerbaijan (at the time, part of thee U.S.S.R.). At the age of five he learned the moves of chess just by watching his father play. He progressed rapidly. At this time the Soviet Union, with its strong chess tradition, was the best place in the world for a talented chess player to grow up. From an early age, Kasparov was able to receive first-class instruction. His rise to the top of the chess world was meteoric.

This was the final position from the 24th and final game of the 1985 match. Kasparov (Black) has just moved his knight away from the c2 square so that the rook checks Karpov's king—a classic case of a discovered check. At this point, Karpov resigned the game and with it the chess crown. When White's king moves, the knight will capture White's rook on e6, leaving Black in a winning position.

▽ At the age of 19, Kasparov already had a charismatic presence at the board, impressing his opponents with his enormous confidence and sheer will to win.

KASPAROV'S STYLE

When Garry Kasparov arrived on the international chess scene in the late 1970s and early 1980s, he was completely unstoppable. He didn't just beat the opposition, he destroyed it. Most chess in the 1970s had been about grinding down one's opponent without taking risks. Kasparov's play was completely different—dynamic, explosive, and fearless.

△ In the 1993 World Championship match, Kasparov faced a new challenger—the English player, Nigel Short.

CAREER RECORD

1963	Born in Baku, in the Soviet Republic of Azerbaijan.
1968	Learns the moves of chess.
1975	U.S.S.R. Junior Champion.
1980	World Junior Champion; gains Grandmaster title.
1984	First challenges Karpov for the world title.
1985	Match abandoned in February after five months due to Karpov's exhaustion.
1985	Kasparov wins rematch six months later to become youngest World Champion ever at 22.
1986	Defeats Karpov in London and Leningrad . . .
1987	. . . and again in Seville
1990	. . . and again in New York and Lyons.
1993	A new challenger, Nigel Short, is defeated.
1995	Defends title against Anand in New York.
1997	Defeated by *Deep Blue* in New York.
2000	Loses world title to Kramnik in London.
2005	Retires from chess, having won every major title.

THE SOVIET OUTSIDER

Chess and politics were always closely bound up in the Soviet Union. For the Soviet authorities, the outspoken Kasparov was a concern. In his first World Championship encounter with Anatoly Karpov in 1984, the Soviet Sports Committee halted the match when it looked as though the exhausted Karpov—their loyal favorite—was crumbling. One Soviet bureaucrat said at the time, "We have one World Champion, we don't need another," especially if it was going to be one who chose not to follow the party line.

In 1990, Kasparov fled his home in Baku, on the Caspian Sea, when Azeri nationalists took over the city. He chartered a plane from Moscow to bring out as many people as possible from the threatened Armenian community.

After retiring from chess, Kasparov entered the turbulent world of Russian politics. A fierce critic of President (now Prime Minister) Vladimir Putin, he has not found life as easy as on the chessboard. In 2007, he spent five days in prison for leading a protest march demanding fair elections.

THE SHORTEST AND LONGEST GAMES

A game of chess can be decided in just a few moves—or it may take hundreds. And the play can be as quick or as slow as the players wish. One of the most popular forms of chess is "blitz," where both players have a total of five minutes to make all their moves. And for some players even that isn't fast enough . . .

THE SHORTEST GAMES

The quickest checkmate can be achieved in just two moves—but only with a hugely cooperative opponent, so don't get your hopes up. It is no wonder that this checkmate is called Fool's Mate (**diagram 1**).

1 **1 g4 e5 2 f3 Qh4**
Checkmate. The king, boxed in by its own pieces, has no escape. Terrible play from White! At the start of the game pawns should always be advanced from the center of the board, not from the side.

A quick checkmate that is more useful to know about is Scholar's Mate. This attack is not recommended—it can rebound horribly—but you should be aware of it in case someone springs it on you (**diagrams 2, 3, and 4**).

2 **1 e4 e5 2 Bc4**
Sensible opening moves from both sides so far. The pawns advance in the middle and the bishop arrives at a good square.
2 ...Bc5 3 Qh5

3 *Black also plays the bishop out, and White brings the queen into the game, threatening the pawn on e5 and checkmate on f7. If Black moves the queen to e7 both threats would be covered. But instead, Black makes a poor move.*
3 ...Nc6 4 Qxf7

4 *Checkmate. Black spotted that the e-pawn needed to be defended and covered it with the knight, but missed the bigger threat—checkmate on f7. The Black king cannot take the queen because it's supported by the bishop. A checkmate that could have been avoided.*

THE LONGEST GAME

Most modern tournament games now have an imposed time limit of seven hours. Previously there was no limit. In 1989, one game played in serious competition lasted 20 hours and 15 minutes and took 269 moves. And the result of this lengthy game? A draw.

THE MOSCOW MARATHON

The longest World Championship final took place from 1984 to1985 and involved two Soviet players, Anatoly Karpov and Garry Kasparov. The first to win six games would be declared the winner. However, after winning five games, Karpov was unable to finish off Kasparov. At one point, there were 17 draws in a row. Eventually, after 48 games, the match was abandoned, with Karpov suffering from physical and mental exhaustion. In the return match, later in 1985, a maximum limit of 24 games was reintroduced, much to everyone's relief.

◁ The 1984–1985 World Championship final between Karpov (left) and Kasparov (right) lasted a grueling five months. Even the Russian chess public lost patience at one point, booing and wolf whistling at the two players.

CORRESPONDENCE CHESS

One form of chess that breaks all longevity records is correspondence chess. Players mail their moves to each other. They are generally allowed three days to respond. Some games take years to finish. It is not unknown for players to die before a game has been completed!

SPEED CHESS

At the other extreme, the first one-minute world championship ("bullet chess") was organized in 1999. The rules are simple—you have to play ALL your moves in one minute, or you lose the game. (If you are interested, check out the Internet Chess Club at www.chessclub.com.)

STARERS AND SHAKERS

Such are the passions aroused by chess that, occasionally, some players even break the rules in order to win. However, much more common than outright cheating is "gamesmanship." This is the art of unsettling your opponent, but staying within the rules of the game. As long ago as 1561, Ruy Lopez, one of the best players of his age, suggested positioning the board so that the sun shines in your opponent's eyes!

△ In 1977, the Soviet player Tigran Petrosian had a bruising encounter with the Soviet defector Viktor Korchnoi, involving table-shaking and the use of feet!

UNSPORTING BEHAVIOR?

A fairly common tactic is for a player to develop certain exaggerated mannerisms at the board. You might recognize the following types.

The **piece-thumper** will smash a piece down right in the heart of your army, usually to distract your attention from another part of the board.

The **smug opponent** will cast a bemused look at your move, and follow with a quick reply and an amused smile.

The **starer** is more intimidating. World Champion Mikhail Tal's penetrating stare unnerved one opponent so much that he countered by wearing reflective sunglasses.

The **table-shaker** can be equally unsettling. It is difficult to concentrate properly when the pieces are wobbling. Tigran Petrosian used this tactic against Viktor Korchnoi in 1977. Korchnoi asked him to stop, but Petrosian responded by turning off his hearing aid. Korchnoi replied with a swift kick under the table. For the next game a partition was built under the table.

PUSHING THE LIMITS

The chess match that inspired the most gamesmanship was the 1978 World Championship final between Anatoly Karpov, representing the Soviet Union, and Viktor Korchnoi, who at that time was stateless. Korchnoi had defected from the Soviet Union two years earlier. Under such politically charged circumstances, there was always going to be enormous tension during the match.

CODED YOGURTS

In the middle of the second game, Karpov was handed a container of yogurt. Korchnoi's camp issued a formal protest after the game, claiming that the delivery could convey a coded message: "A yogurt after move 20 could signify, 'We instruct you to offer a draw'. The possibilities are limitless." After this, it was decreed that Karpov could only have a particular flavor of yogurt and that it should be served at a specific time by a designated waiter.

MIND GAMES

A Soviet parapsychologist, Dr. Vladimir Zukhar, sat at the front of the audience staring directly at Korchnoi for the entire game. One of Korchnoi's delegation counteracted the possibility of undue mental interference by handing Dr. Zukhar a copy of the anti-Soviet novel *The Gulag Archipelago*, then sat behind him for the rest of the game prodding him with a ballpoint pen.

For the record, Karpov won the match.

△ *During the 1978 World Championship final, Viktor Korchnoi (right) alleged that Anatoly Karpov's team employed underhanded tactics.*

THE RUSSIANS AND CHESS

Chess reached Russia from Persia in the 800s. As in other countries, until the 1900s, chess in Russia was mainly a game for intellectuals and the wealthy. But after the October Revolution of 1917, chess gripped the Soviet Union's vast population as a result of an extraordinary and unique social experiment.

△ The Soviet Union was the world's first Communist country. It was founded in 1922, four years after the Bolsheviks, headed by Lenin, seized power.

△ Nikolai Krylenko initiated a major program for the development of chess in the Soviet Union.

CHESS AND COMMUNISM

After the Communists came to power they were faced with the challenge of educating the people in the principles of Marxism, the political and economic theories on which the Soviet Union was based. By promoting chess, the government hoped to instill the rudiments of scientific, rational thinking in its people and weaken the grip of the Russian Orthodox Church, which was considered an enemy of communism.

THE GREAT PLAN

Lenin, the first Communist leader, was an enthusiastic chess player. After he died in 1924, Nikolai Krylenko, Commissar for War in the first Communist government, helped popularize chess. Soon there were chess clubs in factories and schools all over the country. When young players showed talent, they were given special instruction. Krylenko's ambitious program was a great success. By 1936, 700,000 players took part in the Soviet Trade Union championship. In the early 1970s, there were some four million registered chess players in the Soviet Union.

△ During the 1930s, chess clubs were formed across the Soviet Union— in factories and libraries, on farms, and in the army.

VORKERS!"

"EVERY CHESS-PLAYING WORKER IN THE U.S.S.R. IS A LEADER OF SOCIALIST COMPETITION IN INDUSTRY."

"CHESS IS A TRUE WEAPON AGAINST RELIGIOUS DELUSIONS."

FIRST SUCCESS

From this mass movement it was inevitable that champions would be produced. The first great international success was Mikhail Botvinnik, who won the famous Nottingham tournament of 1936. In the main Soviet newspaper, *Pravda*, Botvinnik thanked Stalin, "beloved teacher and leader," for inspiring his victory. In the Soviet Union, politics and chess went hand in hand. Botvinnik's success heralded the Soviet domination of world chess after World War II.

△ *Mikhail Botvinnik (left) became the first Soviet World Champion ever in 1948. He was hard-working, logical, and completely loyal to the Communist party.*

SOVIET SUPREMACY

From 1948 until 1972, every single World Champion was Soviet. Success bred more success. Botvinnik set up a chess school based on his methodical approach to the game, from which many players benefited, including future World Champions Anatoly Karpov, Garry Kasparov, and Vladimir Kramnik.

THE FUTURE

With the collapse of the Communist regime in 1991, and with it the breakup of the Soviet Union, state funding for chess virtually disappeared. However, with such a strong chess tradition, excellent players continue to come out of the region, and the world's top 20 is still filled with players from the former Soviet Union.

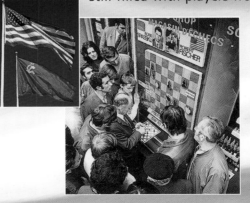

◁ *Struggles on the board, such as the Fischer–Spassky World Championship tournament of 1972, mirrored the intense political rivalry—the Cold War—between the Soviet Union and the United States.*

COMPUTERS AND CHESS

Since the pioneering days of computer science in the 1940s, researchers have developed and constructed chess-playing machines. Not until the late 1980s, however, did computers become powerful enough to take on the strongest players in the world.

◁ *Early computer pioneers, such as Alan Turing, believed that constructing chess-playing programs would be of enormous benefit to their work.*

◁ *In 1769, the Hungarian inventor Baron Wolfgang Von Kemplen exhibited his chess-playing automaton, The Turk. This mechanical figure appeared to move the pieces by itself. It was, in fact, operated by a person concealed inside the lower compartment.*

HOW DOES A COMPUTER PLAY CHESS?

The best human chess players, using intuition, will examine perhaps just two or three moves in a position. After studying them each in turn, the player will decide which one is best.

A computer "thinks" about chess in a very different way. First, it will examine all possible moves in a position and then all the possible moves after those moves, and so on. It doesn't take long before the computer has examined literally millions of different positions. Each position has a pre-programmed value, so the computer can calculate the best move.

While a computer examines far more positions, a human player is much more selective about the number of moves initially considered. Some people argue that humans, therefore, actually look into a position in much greater depth than a computer.

▽ In top chess events, players are scanned before a game to ensure that they have no computer assistance.

Did you know ?

Chess is ideal for playing on the Internet. You can log onto the World Wide Web and find thousands of people all over the world playing chess. If you are interested in playing, turn to page 60 for a list of websites.

◁ *The latest chess computers can play at many different levels and often have famous games pre-programmed in their memory. These machines are an excellent way to improve your game.*

HOW TO BEAT YOUR CHESS COMPUTER

Chess-playing computers of a high caliber are now available to everyone. They present a different kind of challenge to a human opponent. Here are some tips to help you beat your chess computer.

- Start on the lowest level, then build up.
- Computers are brilliant at short-term tactics, so be very careful with your pieces. Watch out for tricks like forks and pins.
- Computers are less good at long-term planning—humans are much better in this respect. For example, if you see a potential weak point on the other side of the board, make sure that you exploit it.
- If all else fails, pull out the plug!

CHESS DATABASES

The computer's capacity to store huge amounts of information has revolutionized chess. Every professional player carries a laptop computer containing millions of games from top-class events. With a couple of keystrokes it's possible to recall the past games of opponents, then search for weaknesses in their play, just as any football coach will study the opposing team's defense on DVD before a game.

◁ *In the 2006 World Championship contest, Veselin Topalov (right) accused Vladimir Kramnik of using computer assistance.*

"If a computer can beat the World Champion, a computer can read the best books in the world, can write the best plays, and can know everything about history and literature and people."
Garry Kasparov, World Chess Champion

THE ULTIMATE CHALLENGE

In May 1997, a chess match took place that would make headlines all over the world. Garry Kasparov, the reigning World Chess Champion, and arguably the greatest player in the history of the game, sat down to face *Deep Blue*, a 1.4-ton computer built and operated by a team of U.S. scientists.

KASPAROV VERSUS *DEEP BLUE*

The *Deep Blue* team tried twice before to defeat Garry Kasparov, in 1989 and 1996. On both occasions the computer had been crushed. In 1997, they met for another six-game match. The IBM team behind *Deep Blue* was confident that their machine was now good enough to defeat the World Champion. However, when Garry Kasparov was asked before the match whether the unthinkable might happen, he replied, "I don't think it is an appropriate thing to discuss whether I might lose. I never lose. I have never lost in my life."

◁ *One of* Deep Blue*'s massive processors. The name* Deep Blue *combines the orginal name of the project,* Deep Thought, *with IBM's nickname,* Big Blue.

△ *Sitting opposite Kasparov (right) is one of the* Deep Blue *team, ready to play the machine's moves as they appear on screen.*

THE BIG FIGHT

As the match progressed it became clear that *Deep Blue* was far stronger than in previous years. Going into the sixth and final game, the scores were even. And then for the first time in his career, Kasparov cracked up. After just one hour—an average game at the top level of chess lasts about four hours—his position lay in ruins. At the closing ceremony Kasparov was livid. He raged that if *Deep Blue* played in a regular tournament, he would "tear it to pieces."

THE CONTENDERS		
Deep Blue		Kasparov
6'5"	Height	5'10"
1.4 tons	Weight	176 lbs
8	Age	34
32 processors	Processors	50 billion neurons
200 million	Moves per second	2
Electrical	Power Source	Electrical/chemical

△ Kasparov feels the heat at various stages during the nine-day match. Throughout the games, he found himself under constant pressure as Deep Blue worked out moves far more quickly than he did.

THE FUTURE

Kasparov had never previously lost a major contest, and he wanted revenge. Unfortunately for him, the *Deep Blue* team disbanded after the match. So should we pack up our chess sets and leave the game to machines? The answer is definitely not. The possibilities of chess are almost endless. *Deep Blue* does not play perfect chess. Even with much more powerful computers, it will be some time, possibly never, before a computer has "solved" the mystery of the game.

△ Kasparov (Black) lost his most powerful piece, the queen. His king is left exposed and is about to be cut down by Deep Blue's pieces. At this point, the human World Champion had had enough. He resigned the game.

GLOSSARY

The following pages contain some common terms used in chess. Not all of these terms are used in this book, but they may be useful if you read other books on the subject.

Blindfold chess A game in which the player cannot see the board—it isn't absolutely necessary to wear a blindfold! Players visualize the positions in their heads and call out their moves using chess notation.

Check A piece that directly attacks the king is said to "give check" or put it "in check." (*See pages 20–21.*)

Checkmate The end of the game, when the king is put in check and cannot escape. (*See pages 20–21.*)

Combination A sequence of moves leading to material gain or checkmate.

Correspondence chess A game of chess played by mail. Moves are recorded in chess notation and sent to the opponent.

Development Bringing pieces out at the start of the game. Having a "lead in development" can be of crucial importance.

Diagonal A line of squares running obliquely (on an angle) across the board, along which both the bishop and the queen are able to move. Diagonals are identified by naming the squares at either end, for instance, the b1–h7 diagonal.

Discovered check When a piece moves, allowing a second piece to give check. (*See pages 32–33.*)

Double attack One piece attacks two pieces at the same time. A knight fork is an example of a double attack.

Double check Two pieces put the king in check at the same time. This occurs when a discovered check is played and both pieces give check.

Endgame or Ending The third phase of the game, after the opening and the middlegame, when just a few pieces remain on the board. Strategy is different from the first two phases. For instance, mating attacks are rare, so the king becomes a powerful piece. Ultimately, the aim is to force a pawn to the eighth rank to get a new queen.

En prise A piece that is attacked but isn't defended is said to be "en prise." Similarly, a piece that is attacked by one less valuable than itself is also "en prise," for example, when a knight attacks a queen. ("Prise" rhymes with "cheese.")

Exchange, an When pieces of equal value are traded off the board. For instance, "a bishop exchange" means that both sides have given up a bishop. (Note that this is different from "the exchange," *see below*.)

Exchange, the This is a trade of particular pieces—a rook for a knight, or a rook for a bishop. If one player has lost a rook or a knight, for example, they are said to be "the exchange down."

Fianchetto The knight's pawn is advanced one square, creating room for the bishop to move on the longest diagonal—on g2 or b2 if you are White, b7 or g7 if you are Black. Although it is at the side of the board, the bishop influences the entire board.

FIDE (Fédération Internationale des Échecs) The world's governing body for chess, founded in 1924 in Paris. FIDE has many responsibilities. It determines the more obscure rules of the game, awards titles such as Master and Grandmaster, and hosts the chess Olympics.

File A line of eight squares running up the board. These vertical columns are often referred to by a letter, for instance, "Black's rooks can enter the position down the c-file."

Flank One side of the board.

Fork When two enemy pieces are attacked by a single piece, usually a knight. (*See pages 30–31.*)

Gambit An opening in which material is given up to gain a lead in development. Usually this is a pawn or two, but sometimes a gambit can involve sacrificing a more important piece such as a knight or a bishop. (*See page 28.*)

Grandmaster Next to World Champion, the highest title in chess. Of the millions of serious players in the world, there are just a few hundred who have been awarded the title "Grandmaster" from FIDE. The full title is actually "International Grandmaster," but this is not used very often.

Initiative If you have the initiative you have more control over the game and can make threats to put your opponent on the defensive. Holding "the initiative" gives you options, but it must be converted into something more tangible.

International Master The next title down from Grandmaster.

Isolated pawn A pawn is said to be isolated if there are no pawns of its own color on adjacent files. In other words, it cannot be protected by another pawn, so, in theory at least, it is more vulnerable to attack.

Kingside The half of the board on which the king stands at the beginning of the game. In other words, the right-hand side of the board from White's point of view. Even if the king moves away to the left, the kingside remains the half of the board where the king was standing at the beginning. (*See* Queenside.)

Major piece A queen or a rook.

Material A term for pieces, often used in a more general sense when discussing values. For example, "White loses material" means that White loses more pieces than Black.

Middlegame The second of the three phases of the game. All pieces have been developed, and the real battle has begun. (*See* Opening *and* Endgame.)

Minor piece A knight or a bishop.

Open file A file on which there are no pawns, making it possible for a rook or a queen to penetrate deep into the enemy position. Sometimes controlling the only "open file" is enough for a player to force a win.

Opening, an A planned system at the beginning of the game.

Opening, the The first phase of the game. Pieces are brought out and the king finds safety. (*See pages 28–29.*)

Passed pawn A pawn that has no enemy pawn in front of it or on an adjacent file. Potentially, this gives the pawn a free run to the eighth rank, where it can become a queen.

Pin A piece is attacked but cannot move because a piece behind it, usually of greater value, would be taken. (*See pages 30–31.*)

Problem A composed position with a set number of moves to force a win or a draw.

Promotion When a pawn reaches the eighth rank it may turn into any other piece—knight, bishop, rook, or queen. Because the queen is so powerful, other pieces are rarely selected. (*See page 17.*)

Queenside The half of the board on which the queen stands at the start of the game—from White's point of view, the left-hand side of the board. Even if the queen moves to the other half of the board, the queenside remains the half of the board where the queen stood at the beginning of the game. (*See* Kingside.)

Rank The rows of squares that run across the board, denoted by the numbers 1 to 8.

Resignation A player, knowing that defeat is inevitable, gives up the game before checkmate occurs.

Sacrifice When material is given up in order to gain an advantage in the long run. (*See pages 34–35.*)

Score sheet The official document on which moves are recorded during a game. All tournament games must be recorded—it is part of the official rules of chess.

Simultaneous exhibition An event in which a Grandmaster or expert takes on a number of weaker players at once. Usually up to 30 players are taken on, but the record is reputedly held by a Yugoslav chess journalist, Dmitri Bjelica, who played 301 players simultaneously in 1982. The display lasted 9 hours—he won 258, drew 36, and lost 7.

Skewer When two pieces are attacked along the same line. Usually, the most valuable piece is attacked first. After this piece has moved, the piece of lesser value behind it is captured.

Stalemate When the player whose turn it is cannot make any legal moves but is not in check. The game ends as a draw. (*See page 37.*)

Strategy Long-term planning.

Tactics This has a distinct meaning in chess. A tactic is a short-term operation, usually played to win material. The more common tactics have acquired colorful names such as "skewer."

Tempo, tempi A unit of time expressed in terms of a move. For instance, if the queen advances, but then has to retreat on the next turn, it could be said that a tempo has been lost (one move). If several tempi have been lost, then several moves have been wasted.

Time trouble All serious tournament games are played within a time limit, using a special chess clock. The standard time limit for tournament games is 40 moves in 2 hours for each player, followed by another 20 moves in 1 hour if the game is unfinished. When players mishandle their time allocation and must make several moves quickly to reach the required number of moves, they are said to be "in time trouble" or "under time pressure." Some players are time pressure addicts, who seem able to move only with the rush of adrenaline that comes when the clock approaches zero hour.

Under-promotion When a pawn reaches the eighth rank, but a piece other than the queen is selected.

Zugzwang A German word meaning "compulsion to move." Occasionally a situation occurs in which any move will compromise the player's position. It would be better to "pass," but this is not allowed.

ANSWERS AND RESOURCES

ANSWERS TO PAGES 12–16

Page 12: The king can take the knight on d6, the pawn on d7, or the rook on f8.

Page 13: The rook can capture either the pawn on d6 or the knight on c1.

Page 14: The bishop is only able to capture one piece: the pawn on a2.

Page 15: The queen can capture the rook on e7, the knight on b6, or the pawn on f2.

Page 16: The knight can capture the pawn on e3, the bishop on b4, or the rook on c7.

TEST POSITIONS, PAGES 40–41

 Black should promote to a queen with **1 ...e1(Q)**—*which actually puts White in checkmate.*

2 *By far the best move is to play* **1 ...Nxg3**, *winning a bishop at no cost. It is illegal for White to capture the knight with the pawn—this would put the king in check from the bishop on b6.*

CONTACTS

America's Foundation for Chess
http://af4c.memfirstclubs.net

Chess Federation of Canada
www.chess.ca

FIDE (World Chess Federation)
www.fide.com

National Scholastic Chess Foundation
www.nscfchess.org

North American Chess Association
www.nachess.org

U.S. Chess Federation
www.uschess.org

THE INTERNET

There are many websites dedicated to playing chess, as well as other aspects of the game: news, opinion, instruction, and online stores.

*At the Internet Chess Club (***www.chessclub.com***) and Play Chess (***www.playchess.com***), you can play online (mainly speed chess), follow top tournaments live, listen to lectures, and read tutorials. Both charge a small annual subscription.*

The Free Internet Chess Server is mostly a no-fee playing site, but you can also watch events online: **www.freechess.org**

www.chessgames.com *is for players who enjoy a slower time limit. You can set the clock, for example, at one move per day. It also has an archive of games if you want to research the techniques of the world's best players.*

*Chess is included at MSN's gaming zone (***www.zone.com***) and also at* **www.yahoo.com**.

3 *The best way to meet the threat from White is to move the king away from the middle as quickly as possible by castling:* **1 ...0–0.** *Tucked behind the pawns, Black's king is fairly safe.*

4 *White should capture the pawn in the middle with the bishop:* **1 Bxd5,** *exploiting the pin. If the bishop is captured* **1 ...Bxd5,** *then White takes the rook with* **2 Rxa7.** *If it isn't captured, then White will take the bishop on b7. In either case, White has a winning material advantage.*

5 *White can play* **1 Rh3+,** *skewering king and rook. Black's king must move, for instance:* **1 ...Kf2.** *White can then capture the rook on the other side of the board:* **2 Rxa3.**

6 *Black can checkmate in one move:* **1 ...Qh2** *mate.*

7 *White has a lethal discovered check:* **1 Rf2+.** *Black's king must move out of the check from the bishop:* **1 ...Kg8,** *then White takes the queen,* **2 Rxg2,** *giving a decisive material advantage.*

8 *There is more than one good move here, but the best is to sacrifice the queen with* **1 Qxc5+.** *If Black plays* **1 ...Qxc5,** *then White delivers a crushing blow with* **2 Bxa6** *checkmate.*

9 *White has a very sneaky way to win from this position. White plays* **1 g8(Q)+.** *Black, of course, must capture the new queen:* **1 ...Kxg8.** *But then comes a knight fork:* **2 Ne7+.** *After Black's king moves out of check, the knight takes the rook. With an extra knight, White should be able to win the game.*

10 *White can still draw the game with this amazing defense:* **1 Qg8+.** *Black must capture the queen,* **1 ...Kxg8,** *but then White has no legal move. Since White is not in check, the position is stalemate—a draw.*

INDEX

A
Alekhine, Alexander 42, 43
algebraic system, notation 18-19
Anand, Viswanathan 43, 45
Arabs 7

B
back rank mate 33
bishop 8, 14
    back rank mate 33
    bishop pair 14
    diagonal battery 32
    moves 14
    notation 19
    opening the game 28
    pawn forks 30, 31
    pin 31
    setting up 10
    value 25
blindfold chess 58
blitz 48
Botvinnik, Mikhail 42, 43, 45, 53
bullet chess 49

C
Capablanca, José-Raoul 42, 43
castle see rook
castling 13, 26-27, 29
Caxton, William 9
check 20-23, 58
    discovered check 32-33, 46, 58

double check 58
checkmate 12, 20-23, 36, 58
    back rank mate 33
    Fool's Mate 48
    sacrifice 34
    Scholar's Mate 48
    "seventh heaven" 33
    training exercises 38-39
chess clubs 52
China 9
combination 58
communism 52-53
computers 9, 54-57
correspondence chess 49, 58

D
Deep Blue 47, 56-57
development 58
diagonal 58
diagonal battery 32
discovered check 32-33, 46, 58
distracting techniques 50
double attack 58
double check 58
draws 36-37

E
Egypt 6
elephants 14
endgame 25, 58
en passant 27
en prise 58
Euwe, Max 42, 43
exchange 58

F
fianchetto 58
FIDE (Fédération Internationale des Échecs) 45, 58, 60
fifty-move rule 37
files 18, 58
Fischer, Bobby 43, 53
flank 58
Fool's Mate 48
fork 30-31, 58

G
gambits 28, 58
gamesmanship 50-51
Germany 9
Grandmasters 58

H
history of chess 7-9

I
IBM 56
India 6, 7, 14, 15, 16, 45
initiative 58
International Masters 59
Internet 55, 60
Islam 7
Isle of Lewis chess pieces 7
isolated pawns 59
Italy 8, 9

K
Karpov, Anatoly 43, 44, 46, 47, 49, 51, 53
Kasparov, Garry 7, 43, 45,

46-47, 49, 53, 56-57
Khalifman, Alexander 45
king 12
    back rank mate 33
    castling 26-7, 29
    check 20-23
    checkmate 12, 20-3, 36, 38-39
    diagonal battery 32
    discovered check 32-33, 46
    draws 36
    knight fork 31
    material chess 24
    moves 12
    notation 19
    pin 31
    setting up 10-11
    "seventh heaven" 33
    skewer 31
    stalemate 37
    training exercises 39
kingside 59
kingside castling 26
knight 8, 16
    discovered check 32-33, 46
    fork 30, 31
    moves 16
    notation 19
    opening the game 28
    pawn fork 31
    pin 31
    sacrifice 34
    setting up 10
    skewer 31
    value 25

Korchnoi, Viktor 27, 44, 50, 51
Krylenko, Nikolai 52
Kramnik, Vladimir 43, 45, 46, 53, 55

L
Lasker, Emanuel 42, 43
Lenin 52
London 9
long castling 26
"long diagonal" 32
longest games 49
Lopez, Ruy 50

M
major pieces 59
material chess 24-25, 59
Middle Ages 8
middlegame 59
minor pieces 59

N
names of pieces 8
notation 18-19

O
open file 59
openings 28-29, 59

P
Paris 9
passed pawns 59
pawns 8, 17
    back rank mate 33
    draws 36
    en passant 27
    fifty-move rule 37

fork 30, 31
gambits 28
isolated pawns 59
moves 17
opening the game 28
passed pawns 59
pin 31
promotion 17, 25, 59
setting up 11
"seventh heaven" 33
stalemate 37
training exercises 39
value 25
Persia 7, 15, 20, 52
Petrosian, Tigran 43, 44, 50
Philidor, André 17
piece-thumpers 50
pin 30-31, 59
promotion 17, 25, 59

Q
queen 8, 15
    back rank mate 33
    checkmate 36, 38-39
    diagonal battery 32
    discovered check 32-33
    knight fork 31
    moves 15
    notation 19
    opening the game 28, 29
    pin 30, 31
    promotion 17, 25, 59
    sacrifice 34
    setting up 10-11
    skewer 31
    stalemate 37
    value 25
queenside 59

queenside castling 26

R
ranks 18, 59
Renaissance 8, 9
repetition of position 36-37
resignation 59
rook 13
    back rank mate 33
    castling 13, 26-27, 29
    checkmate 36, 38
    discovered check 32-33, 46
    moves 13
    notation 19
    pin 30
    sacrifice 35
    setting up 10
    "seventh heaven" 33
    skewer 31
    value 25
Russia 14, 52-53

S
sacrifice 34-35, 59
Scholar's Mate 48
score sheets 59
setting up 10-11
short castling 26
shortest games 48, 49
Sicily 7
simultaneous exhibitions 59
skewer 30-31, 59
smug opponent 50
Smyslov, Vassily 42, 43
Soviet Union 9, 47, 52-53
Spain 7, 8, 9
Spassky, Boris 43, 44

special moves 26-27
stalemate 37, 59
Stalin, Joseph 53
starers 50
Steinitz, Wilhelm 42, 43
strategy 59

T
tactics 59
Tal, Mikhail 34, 43, 50
tempo 59
test positions 40-41
time limits 49, 59
Topalov, Veselin 55
tournaments
    draws 36, 37
    longest games 49
    World Championship 42-45, 49, 51, 53
training exercises 38-39
Turing, Alan 54

U
under-promotion 59

V
value of pieces 24-25
Vikings 7

W
William the Conqueror 12
World Championship 42-47, 49, 51, 53

Z
Zugzwang 59
Zukertort, Johannes 42
Zukhar, Dr. Vladimir 51

ACKNOWLEDGMENTS

The publishers would like to thank the following illustrators for their contribution to this book: **Julie Hartigan** 42-43, 48-49, 54-55; all other illustrations created by **Mike Buckley**.

The publishers would like to thank the following for supplying photographs:

6 l AKG London/British Museum, London, tc The Art Archive, bc AKG London/British Museum, London; 7 tc The Bridgeman Art Library/British Library, London, r AKG London/British Museum, London, bl The Bridgeman Art Library/Musée Condé, Chantilly, France; 8 tl The Art Archive/Bibliothèque Nationale Paris, cl AKG London/Erich Lessing, bl Christies Images, b Christies Images; 8-9 bl Christies Images; 9 tr Mary Evans Picture Library, cr The Kobal Collection, br Mattel Interactive; 42 tl Mary Evans Picture Library; tcl (Lasker) Hulton Getty; tc (Capablanca) Hulton Getty; tc (Alekhine) Hulton Getty; tcr (Euwe) Hulton Getty; tr (Botvinnik) Society for Cooperation in Russian and Soviet Studies (SCR) Photo Library Photo Library/Novosti; tr (Smyslov) Topham Picture Point; 43 tcl (Tal) SCR/Novosti; t (Petrosian) SCR Photo Library/Novosti; tc (Spassky) SCR Photo Library/Novosti; tc (Fischer) Topham Picture Point; tc (Karpov) Topham Picture Point; tr (Kasparov) SCR Photo Library/Novosti; tr (Kramnik) Rex Features/Sipa Press; tr (Anand) Reuters/Pawel Kopczynski; 45 tr Sovfoto; cr Cathy Rogers; bl Getty Images/AFP/Tauseef Mustafa; 46 tl SCR Photo Library/Novosti, tc SCR Photo Library/Novosti, bc Topham Picture Point/Associated Press; 46-47 t IBM; 47 c Allsport UK Ltd/Chris Cole; 49 tc SCR Photo Library/Novosti; 50 c SCR Photo Library/Novosti; 50-51 repeat image in digital a/w SCR Photo Library/Novosti; 51 tl Hulton Getty; 52 tl SCR Photo Library, cl Hulton Getty, bl SCR Photo Library; 53 tr SCR Photo Library, bl Frank Spooner Pictures/D. Kennerly-Liaison, bc Hulton Getty; 54 tr Science Photo Library, cl AKG London; 55 55 tl Cathy Rogers; b PA/AP; 56 c Rex Features, bl Popperfoto/Jeff Christensen/Reuters; 57 tl (*Deep Blue*) Frank Spooner Pictures/Swanson/Liaison, tl Rex Features/Andre Camara, tc Rex Features/Erik Pendzich, tr (*Deep Blue*) Popperfoto/Peter Morgan/Reuters, tr Rex Features/Erik Pendzich.

Key: b = bottom, c = center, l=left, t = top, r = right.

Every effort has been made to trace the copyright holders of the photographs. The publishers apologize for any inconvenience caused.

The author would like to thank Mairéad, Declan, and Kathryn.